Bare Root
MORNINGS

Brunch Recipes for the
Modern Food Lover

RECIPES & PHOTOGRAPHY BY ANGELA GALLARDO

First Edition 2015
ISBN (paperback): 978-1-5120-6643-2

CONTENTS

ABOUT BARE ROOT GIRL

BareRootGirl.com and the Bare Root cookbooks are an endeavor to unite the modern food lover in me with my passion for Primal.

My story began in 2007 when I spent 6 months living outside the US for the first time. I taught English at a bilingual school in a rural town high in the mountains of Honduras. It was a true adventure, both excitingly refreshing and just a little dangerous -- to my health, that is.

The effect on my health was significant. Thanks to a bout of gastroenteritis that occurred from eating contaminated food, I came home with a parasite infection and a host of accompanying issues due to the poor sanitation where I lived. Prior to the trip, I'd considered myself a pretty healthy person. But I was not *(yet)* armed with the knowledge I needed to get back to full health. Severe digestive distress, chronic fatigue, joint pain akin to a 65-yo woman, insomnia, and erratic hormonal behavior are just some of the symptoms that plagued me daily. I saw a number of doctors that couldn't help, and either prescribed antibiotics or told me flat out that food wouldn't help me heal so it didn't matter what I ate.

My awareness of the Paleo/Primal lifestyle came about slowly. An avid cook from a young age, I felt it was far too limiting to let my passion for good food flourish. So I brushed it aside. But through years of struggle -- with a worsening of my symptoms, chronic ovarian cysts, and a miscarriage under my belt -- I learned that a generalized "whole foods diet" with a "moderation in everything" approach was not going to provide me healing.

In February 2014, an exploratory laparoscopy involved the removal of a large benign mass near my left ovary and a diagnosis of endometriosis. Recovery was rough and led to a large amount of self-reflection. I came to the conclusion that no piece of bread or bowl of pasta was worth this suffering and I plunged headfirst into a strict Paleo diet.

The approach I've taken to Paleo is about replacing nutrient-poor foods with nutrient-dense foods. For me, it's not about subscribing religiously to a Paleo dogma or creating lists of 'ok' and 'not ok' foods. It's about eliminating foods that current research tells us are harmful and incorporating foods that our bodies respond well to.

Nearly 8 years after that initial infection in Honduras, I can finally say that I am nearly symptom-free. Follow-up scans have showed no ovarian cysts or regrowth of endometrial tissue. Filling my diet with nutrient-dense foods has allowed my body to finally begin to heal and to function as it was meant to.

I believe whole-heartedly that everyone can find a Paleo model that works and that it can cure many of the ailments plaguing our society today.

~ Angela Gallardo

INTRO TO BARE ROOT MORNINGS

I started *BareRootGirl.com* to challenge myself to create recipes that were not just delicious, but nutrient-dense as well. The positive response I received motivated me to begin a collection of cookbooks -- available in both e-copy and paperback -- that will serve as inspiration for others to unite a Paleo/Primal diet with modern 'fine food' eating. "Bare Root Mornings" is the second book in this series.

Quality ingredients promote maximum flavor in every recipe included here. Everything from investigating the proper handling of raw ingredients to the precisely lowest amount of sweetener a recipe needs to be appealing were given a great deal of consideration. And because food is truly lovely, I tried to let the finished products shine in their natural beauty with a picture for every single recipe.

Knowing that many people who will use this book are dealing with food allergies or intolerances, I've made an effort to include recipes that can be made egg-free, dairy-free, and nut-free. And aside from the recipes found in the Sweet Starts section (which are great for special occasions or a relaxing weekend brunch), most are very low-glycemic.

The approach I've taken with these recipes reflects back to my personal approach to the lifestyle, which is focusing on the nutrient density of the ingredients. Though not noted specifically throughout the book, I highly recommend sourcing organic produce, pastured meat and eggs, wild-caught fish, and soy-free, non-GMO ingredients whenever possible.

I feel strongly that the selection of recipes here in **Bare Root Mornings** provides the foundation for a nutritious, healing diet. All recipes are 100% my original creations. And as many of them took quite a number of attempts to perfect, I'm pretty excited for you to try them.

Are you on Instagram? Tag your photos **#barerootmornings** to show off your recreations!

Crispy Chicken and Waffles, pg. 15

PUT AN EGG ON IT

(or leave it off!)

A teriyaki bowl is within your Paleo-eating reach! Sweet pear marinade tenderizes the meat and allows for a dark caramelization. An easy homemade teriyaki sauce spices up your every day cauli-rice.

TERIYAKI CAULI-RICE

2	small heads cauliflower
2 Tbsp.	avocado oil
3 Tbsp.	extra-virgin sesame oil
2 Tbsp.	coconut aminos
2 Tbsp.	rice vinegar or apple cider vinegar
1 Tbsp.	pure tamarind paste
1 tsp.	honey
1 Tbsp.	freshly grated ginger
1	garlic clove, *minced*
1/2 tsp.	sea salt
1/4 tsp.	black pepper

BULGOGI BEEF

1 lb.	sirloin, denver, or ribeye steak, *sliced thin*
1	pear, *cored & roughly chopped*
3 Tbsp.	avocado oil
2 Tbsp.	coconut aminos
3	garlic cloves
2 Tbsp.	freshly grated ginger
1 tsp.	sea salt
1/2 tsp.	black pepper

THE BOWL

1	medium zucchini, *julienned*
1/2	red onion, *sliced thin*
1	lime, *juiced*
2	baby bok choy, *chopped*
1/2 c.	bone broth or stock of choice
2 tsp.	sesame seeds
4	eggs
	Sea Vegetable Kimchi *(pg. 56)*

Directions:

1. Marinate the Bulgogi Beef by combining the pear, avocado oil, coconut aminos, garlic, ginger, sea salt, and pepper in a blender. Blend until smooth and add to a large ziplock bag with the sliced beef. Marinate for 8 - 12 hours.
2. Prepare the Teriyaki Cauli-rice by chopping the cauliflower and adding the florets to a large food processor fitted with the regular chopping blade (you could also use the shredding attachment or just a regular box grater). Pulse in batches until the cauliflower is broken up into small, rice-like pieces. Dump the riced cauliflower onto a large baking sheet and drizzle with the avocado oil. Bake at 425F for 15-20 minutes, removing the pan halfway to toss the cauliflower.
3. While the cauliflower is baking, combine the extra-virgin sesame oil, coconut aminos, rice vinegar, tamarind paste, honey, grated ginger, minced garlic, sea salt, and black pepper in a large bowl. Whisk until smooth and glossy. When the cauliflower is finished roasting, add it to the teriyaki sauce and stir well.
4. Combine the julienned zucchini and sliced onion in a bowl with the lime juice. Toss and set aside.
5. Heat a large skillet over high heat. Remove the beef slices from the marinade, shake off the excess juices, and add them to the hot pan. Cook in batches until browned on both sides. After the beef is finished, turn the heat to medium. Add the bok choy and bone broth and cook until the bok choy is wilted and most of the liquid is gone. Remove the bok choy from the pan and toss in the sesame seeds. Then use the hot pan to fry the eggs to your desired doneness.
6. Assemble the bowls by layering the cauli-rice, vegetables, beef, egg, and kimchi, as desired.

KOREAN BULGOGI BOWL

Yields: 4 bowls

HUEVOS RANCHEROS
with Plantain Tortillas

Flourless tortillas topped with chorizo, sweet potatoes, peppers, eggs, and a creamy cilantro lime sauce.

PLANTAIN TORTILLAS

1.5 lb.	yellow plantains (about 2 large)*
1/2 c.	fresh lime juice
4 Tbsp.	melted lard, tallow, ghee, or coconut oil
1/2 tsp.	baking soda
	sea salt & black pepper

CILANTRO LIME SAUCE

4 Tbsp.	mayo (homemade, if possible)
1/2	lime, juiced
1 Tbsp.	cilantro, chopped
1	garlic clove, minced

TO ASSEMBLE

8	eggs
1	Chorizo Hash Recipe (pg.48)
	Spicy Salsa Sauerkraut (pg.52)
	avocado, for serving

Tortilla Directions:

1. Preheat the oven to 375F. Line a baking sheet with parchment paper.
2. Chop the plantains and add them to a high-powered blender. Pour in the lime juice and blend at a low speed to break the plantains up. Stop and scrape the sides down. Blend again on low until the mix is smooth and there are no lumps present. Add the melted lard and baking soda and blend again to incorporate. It should resemble baby food (yum!).
3. Scoop the dough out onto the pan with a large-size cookie scoop and use the back of a spoon to smooth it out into circles. Shape to about 4-6" in diameter and 1/4" thickness. You will get about 8 tortillas so it's recommended to fit 4 per baking sheet baked in 2 batches.
4. Bake for 8 minutes and remove the pan from the oven. With a wide spatula, carefully flip the tortillas over. Cook for another 6 minutes, or until they just barely start to turn golden.
5. Sprinkle with sea salt and pepper and let them cool slightly before using. If not using immediately, cover with a tea towel to keep them pliable. You can make a bigger batch and reheat by warming in a skillet or the oven on low heat (they reheat well!).

*Notes:
• I highly recommend using ripe, yellow-skinned plantains. Medium ripe plantains (the skins are usually a combo or green and yellow) will work but it will be more difficult to blend into a smooth dough and the tortillas will be a bit chewier.
• To get a crisper, more "tostada-like" tortilla, overcook them for about 5-8 minutes at the tail-end of the cook time and they will cool crispy like a chip. The tortillas shown here were cooked this way.

Cilantro Lime Sauce Directions:

1. Whisk all ingredients together until smooth. More lime juice may be needed to thin out thicker mayo; adjust to your desired consistency.

Note: for dairy-free, substitute coconut cream for the mayo.

To Assemble:

1. Fry the eggs in a skillet over medium heat, covering with a lid for about 3 minutes for over easy, 5 minutes for medium, and 7 minutes for hard yolks.
2. Assemble the Huevos Rancheros by laying down a warm tortilla, adding the desired amount of the Chorizo Hash, and topping with a fried egg. Garnish with Spicy Salsa Sauerkraut, fresh avocado, and Cilantro Lime Sauce, as desired.

These fun stacks come with a lot of creative freedom. Prepare them as listed here or swap out layers for whatever you have fresh. I love to add cucumber slices, arugula, or turn that avocado into guacamole.

8 oz.	cherry tomatoes
	avocado oil
	sea salt & black pepper
1/2 lb.	slab bacon*
4	whole onion slices, *1/4" thick*
4 c.	dark leafy greens *(spinach, kale, or chard)*
2	garlic cloves, *minced*
1/2 c.	bone broth or stock of choice
4	eggs
2 Tbsp.	white vinegar
1	ripe avocado, *sliced*
	Herbed Hollandaise *(pg. 60)*
1/2	Sweet Potato Fritters recipe *(pg. 45)*

Yields: 4 bennys

Directions:

1. Line a baking sheet with parchment paper. Add the whole cherry tomatoes and drizzle with avocado oil, sea salt, and black pepper. Cook at 275F for 1 hour, rolling the tomatoes around the pan about halfway through. (Optionally, you can skip the roasting and layer your benny with fresh chopped cherry tomatoes.)

2. Heat a large skillet over medium heat. Slice the bacon to 1/4"-thick strips and sear both sides until browned. Remove to a paper towel to rest.

3. Add the onion slices to the hot bacon grease, aiming to keep the whole slice intact while sautéing. Cook until browned on both sides, taking care when flipping. Set the cooked onion onto the paper towel to catch grease.

4. While the onion is browning, heat a medium saucepan over medium low heat on a separate stovetop burner. Add enough water to fill the pan 2/3 of the way full and add the white vinegar. Bring the water to a simmer while finishing cooking the other toppings.

5. After removing the onion from the sauté pan, add the greens and sauté until wilted. Add the garlic and bone broth and continue to cook until most of the liquid has evaporated. Move the pan off the heat until ready to stack.

6. To poach the eggs: crack one egg into a small bowl. With a large spoon, swirl the simmering vinegar water to create a small "tornado" in the middle. Gently pour the egg into the center while the water is still swirling. Cook until the white has visibly solidified and when prodded with a slotted spoon, the yolk still appears runny, about 4-6 minutes. Remove the egg onto a paper towel to catch any excess water. You can cover with a bowl to keep the egg warm. Repeat the process with the rest of the eggs.

7. To prepare your benny stacks: layer the fritter as the base, then stack with the bacon, wilted greens, sautéed onion, avocado slices, roasted tomatoes, poached egg, and Herbed Hollandaise.

*Note: if you ask, most butcher counters will sell bacon as "slab bacon" – which is simply bacon that hasn't been sliced. Slicing bacon to your own desired thickness makes this recipe extra special, but don't forgo the recipe entirely if all you have access to is the regular, thinly-sliced stuff.

A little twist on the classic Steak Tartare. Chilled steak sears golden brown on the outside, while leaving the inside rare. A perfect match for a poached egg and fresh gremolata: a spicy, briny mix of lemon and herbs.

Directions:

1. Pat the steak dry and season it generously with sea salt and black pepper on all sides. Put the seasoned steak in the freezer for 30 minutes.
2. Prepare the Caper Gremolata by combining all the ingredients in a food processor or mortar and pestle. Use the zest of the whole lemon but just a small squeeze of the juice. It should be course in texture and slightly moist. Set it aside to let the flavors merry together (extras of the Gremolata can be stored in the fridge for up to a week).
3. Heat a skillet over high heat (cast iron is recommended for a good sear on your steak). Lightly grease the skillet with high-heat cooking oil and cook the chilled steak on all sides until golden, about 2 minutes per side. Do not add the steak to the pan until it's extremely hot. This dish is best enjoyed with the center rare to offset the briny taste of the Gremolata.
4. Let the steak rest for 5-10 minutes before slicing to keep the juices from running out.
   Serve stacked with arugula, thinly sliced shallots, and Caper Gremolata, as desired.

1/2 lb.	filet, flank or hanger steak
2	poached eggs *(pg. 12)*
1	shallot, *thinly sliced*
	fresh arugula
	sea salt & black pepper

CAPER GREMOLATA

2 c.	fresh parsley, *whole*
1	lemon, *zested (& a bit of juice)*
1 Tbsp.	capers
1 Tbsp.	fresh grated horseradish
2	garlic cloves
pinch	red pepper flakes *(optional)*
2 Tbsp.	extra-virgin olive oil

BREAKFAST STEAK STACK

Yields: 2 servings

Crispy Chicken & WAFFLES

Chicharrones make the perfect grain-free & nut-free breading for crispy pan-fried chicken. They lend a savory flavor that pairs deliciously with waffles and a fried egg.

2	boneless, skinless chicken breasts
3 Tbsp.	tapioca flour (starch)
1/2 tsp.	ground mustard
1/2 tsp.	onion powder
1/2 tsp.	sweet paprika
1/2 tsp.	smoked paprika
1	egg
2 Tbsp.	filtered water
1 1/2 c.	finely crumbled chicharron* (about 3 oz.)
2 Tbsp.	prepared mustard of choice
2 Tbsp.	honey
4	fried eggs
	Avocado oil, lard, or tallow, for pan-frying
	sea salt & black pepper
	Peach & Prosciutto Slaw (pg. 59)
	Browned Butter Waffles (pg. 71)

Yields: 4 servings

Directions:

1. Slice the chicken breasts through the middle so they are half the thickness (similar to butterflying). Pat them dry and set them aside.

2. In a wide, shallow bowl, combine the tapioca flour, ground mustard, onion powder, sweet paprika, and smoked paprika. Stir well.

3. In a separate wide, shallow bowl, whisk together the egg and filtered water.

4. In one last wide, shallow bowl, pour in the crumbled chicharron (a food processor works well to grind them down but you can also place them in a bag and smash them).

5. Set up the bowls in a row: chicken, dry flour mix, wet egg mix, and then chicharron crumbles. Working one piece of chicken at a time, dip the chicken in the flour mix and coat all sides well. Shake off the excess and dip next in the egg mix and coat well. Finally dip into the chicharron crumbles and press it down on both sides of the chicken. Carefully move the coated chicken to a large plate to rest for 5 minutes. Repeat the process with the remaining 3 pieces of chicken.

6. While the chicken breading is resting, heat a medium skillet over medium heat (using a small to medium skillet saves on the oil needed for pan frying). Add high-heat cooking oil to a level of about 1/4" depth in the pan.

7. Pan-fry 1-2 pieces of chicken at a time, careful not to crowd the pan. Cook until the edges show signs of browning, then flip to cook the second side. The thin-ness of the chicken will allow them to cook completely by the time the outside is lightly browned. Move the chicken to a cooling rack to rest for 2-3 minutes before serving. Sprinkle with sea salt and black pepper, to taste.

8. While the chicken is cooking, whisk together the mustard and honey.

9. Layer the chicken with warm Browned Butter Waffles, Peach & Prosciutto Slaw, a fried egg, and honey mustard sauce, as desired (as shown on pg. 6).

*Note: chicharrónes are fried pig skins and can be found in most grocery stores, although try to buy pastured if you can. If you don't have access to chicharrónes, almond meal can be substituted but the crust will not be as crispy.

A morning bowl packed with both flavor and nutrients. Cook the eggs sunny side up so when the yolk breaks, it mixes into the noodles and creates a delicious, creamy sauce.

1	large sweet potato*
2	slices of bacon, *chopped*
1	shallot, *minced*
1/2 lb.	asparagus, *chopped*
2	garlic cloves, *minced*
4	large sea scallops
2	eggs
	fresh chives, *optional for garnish*
	sea salt & black pepper, *to taste*

Directions:

1. Spiralize* the sweet potato and place it in a large bowl.

2. Heat a large skillet over medium heat. Add the bacon and cook until crisp. Remove with a slotted spoon and set it aside on a paper towel. Add the shallot and the asparagus to the hot bacon grease. Sauté until softened, about 3-5 minutes.

3. Add the garlic and the spiralized sweet potato to the pan. Cook until just warmed through, about 2 minutes. Add the crisped bacon back in and stir. Portion the "pasta" into two bowls and set aside.

4. Crack the eggs into the pan. Cover with a lid and cook approximately 3 minutes to over easy, 5 minutes to over medium, and 7 minutes to over hard. Transfer the eggs to the bowls.

5. Turn the heat to medium high. If the pan looks dry, add a bit of high-heat cooking oil. Add the scallops to the pan and cook until golden, about 2 minutes per side. Transfer the scallops to the bowls.

6. Garnish with fresh chives, as desired. Season with sea salt and black pepper, to taste (it won't need much salt due to the saltiness of the bacon).

Notes: A Paderno brand or similar is recommended to better spiralize large, raw sweet potatoes. Use blade 3mm.

If you have a Veggetti or similar, look for smaller, narrow sweet potatoes and use 2 instead of 1 large. You may also need to soften them first by cooking at 400F for 10-15 minutes. Once they're cool enough to handle, use the larger blade side to spiralize.

FOR THE TABLE

One-pot meals that can be served family-style
or prepared ahead for a week of quick breakfasts.

THE TORTILLA

1	large white onion
2 Tbsp.	avocado oil
1/4 c.	ghee, tallow, or lard
2 lb.	yukon gold potatoes
12	eggs
1/2 c.	filtered water
1 sprig	fresh rosemary, *minced*
1/4 t.	ground nutmeg
2 tsp.	sea salt
1 tsp.	black pepper

Directions:

1. Preheat the oven to 400F. Slice the onion and potatoes* to about 1/4" thickness (a mandoline is perfect for even slicing of both; there's no need to peel the potatoes).
2. Add the onion and avocado oil to a 10-12" skillet (oven-safe and non-stick like a cast iron pan). Sauté over medium-low heat until the onions are translucent, about 3-5 minutes. Remove the onions and set them aside. With the heat still on medium low, add the ghee, tallow, or lard (these are recommended for the flavor they lend but coconut oil can also be used) and the potatoes. Toss them to coat. The pan will seem crowded at first but continue to sauté the potatoes, gently tossing them every few minutes. Cook until softened and slightly browned, about 15 minutes.
3. While the potatoes are sautéing, combine the eggs, water, rosemary, nutmeg, sea salt, and pepper. Whisk well to combine. Add the sautéed onion back into the pan and mix them into the potatoes. Pour the egg mix into the pan and move the potatoes around to create an1 even layer on top. Once the edges begin to set, move the pan to the oven.
4. Cook for 10-20 minutes, or until the top is browned (time will vary based on pan size). Invert onto a large platter and top with Romesco Sauce.

Note: if using a skillet smaller than 10", cube the potatoes instead of slicing.

Yields: 6-8 servings

TORTILLA ESPAÑOLA *with Romesco Sauce*

Not really a tortilla at all, this traditional Spanish-style frittata combines pan-fried potatoes with baked egg to create a creamy custard-like bite.

THE ROMESCO SAUCE

8 oz.	cherry tomatoes
1 tsp.	avocado oil
8 oz.	jarred roasted red peppers
1/4 c.	almonds, *roasted*
3	garlic cloves
2 Tbsp.	extra-virgin olive oil
2 tsp.	red wine vinegar
1 tsp.	sea salt
1/2 tsp.	black pepper

Directions:

1. Heat a wide skillet over low heat. Add the whole cherry tomatoes, avocado oil, and a pinch of sea salt to the pan. Shake the pan every couple of minutes to move the tomatoes. Sauté until the skins begin to wilt and show char marks, about 10 minutes.

2. While the tomatoes are sautéing, add the remaining ingredients to the bowl of a large food processor. Pulse a few times to combine. Stop to scrape down the sides.

3. Add the charred tomatoes and pulse again until the desired consistency is reached. It's best enjoyed a little chunky.

4. Serve it fresh overtop the warm Tortilla Española. *(Or make extras and enjoy it over everything -- yes it is <u>that</u> good!)*

CAPICOLA TOMATO TART

Reminiscent of a savory pizza, this light, eggless dish still screams breakfast. A 9" round tart pan with removable base works best for easier slicing after it bakes. Any 9" round or square pan can be used but slicing may be a bit tricky.

1	Crust Recipe *(pg. 24)*
3 Tbsp.	avocado oil
1 Tbsp.	chopped fresh basil
2	garlic cloves, *minced*
1 tsp.	sea salt
1/2 tsp.	black pepper
1/2 lb.	zucchini *(about 1 medium)*
2 lb.	small tomatoes *(about 6)*
3 oz.	capicola *(AKA coppa)*, salami, or soppressata, *thinly sliced*

Yields: 4-6 servings

Directions:

1. Prepare The Crust according to the instructions on page 24 (steps 1-4). While the crust is chilling for 30 minutes, prepare the rest of the tart.

2. Combine the avocado oil, fresh basil, garlic, sea salt, and pepper in a small bowl. Mix it well and set it aside to let the flavors develop.

3. Preheat the oven to 350F.

4. Thinly slice the zucchini to about 1/4" thickness (a mandoline or blade attachment for a food processor are perfect for even slicing). With a serrated knife, slice the tomato to a similar thickness. If possible, try to buy smaller tomatoes that aren't much wider than the zucchini so the slices are similar in width.

5. Once the crust has chilled, prepare the tart by arranging the zucchini, tomato, and capicola in the tart shell. Alternate them in a circular pattern around the outside edge, as shown on page 18. You want them to be packed fairly tight. Complete the filling by creating a small flower shape in the center with a half tomato slice tucked in last.

6. Brush the tart, including the crust, liberally with the basil oil. Bake for 35-45 minutes, or until the crust is golden brown and the tomatoes have a charred appearance. Let the tart cool for 15 minutes before slicing to give the bubbling juices time to seep into the crust.

This recipe is pictured on page 18.

Farmers Market FRITTATA

A meal big on nutrients yet still so satisfying. Sautéing the veggies before adding them in helps to deepen their flavors and make this frittata all the more delicious.

1/2	large white onion
1	small head broccoli
1	small zucchini
1/2	bell pepper
1/2 lb.	asparagus
4	kale, chard, or mustard greens leaves
2 oz.	cherry tomatoes, *halved*
6	eggs
1/4 c.	canned light coconut milk
1/2	lemon, *juiced*
2 Tbsp.	chopped fresh parsley
1 tsp.	sea salt
1/2 tsp.	black pepper

Yields: 4-6 servings

Directions:

1. Preheat the oven to 400F.

2. Heat a large skillet over medium heat. Lightly grease the skillet with high-heat cooking oil. Slice the onion and add it to the hot oil. Cook until the onions have wilted significantly and turned golden, about 10 minutes. Move them out of the skillet and into a large, oven-safe casserole dish, spreading them evenly along the bottom of the pan.

3. While the onions are browning, chop the remaining vegetables into small, evenly-sized pieces. After removing the onions from the skillet, add the broccoli and cook for 3 minutes. Add the zucchini, bell pepper, and asparagus and stir well. Add a bit more oil to the pan if it starts to look dry.

4. Sauté the vegetables until they are soft and start to turn golden, about 10 minutes. Then roughly chop the kale leaves and add them in. Sauté until they are wilted, about 2 minutes. Pour the cooked vegetables into the casserole dish overtop the onions and spread them out evenly.

5. While the vegetables are sautéing, mix the eggs, coconut milk, lemon juice, chopped parsley, sea salt, and black pepper in a large bowl. Whisk well until fluffy and smooth.

6. Pour the eggs overtop the vegetables. Tuck the halved cherry tomatoes in amongst the vegetables and move the dish to the oven.

7. Cook for 20-25 minutes, or until the frittata is puffed up and golden. Cook times will vary depending on the size and depth of your casserole dish.

This recipe is pictured on the title page.

All the popular breakfast meats packed into one dish. And a light, flaky (grain-free!) crust to hold it all together.

THE CRUST

4 tsp.	unflavored grass-fed gelatin
5 Tbsp.	filtered water, *divided*
2 c.	blanched almond flour
1/2 c.	tapioca flour (starch)
1/2 tsp.	sea salt
6 Tbsp.	butter, ghee, lard, tallow, or coconut oil

THE QUICHE FILLING

6	bacon slices
1/2 lb.	Spiced Breakfast Sausage *(pg. 44)*
1/2 lb.	uncured ham, *cubed small*
4	eggs*
1/4 c.	canned light coconut milk
3	scallions, *chopped*
1/2 tsp.	black pepper

Directions:

1. Prepare the crust: combine the gelatin with 4 Tbsp. filtered water in a small bowl. Stir well and set it aside to bloom for 3-5 minutes.

2. Add the almond flour, tapioca flour, and sea salt (omit if using salted butter/ghee) to the bowl of a large food processor. Pulse to combine. Add the bloomed gelatin and process until blended well, at least 60 seconds. Scrape down the sides and turn the flours up from the bottom to ensure the gelatin is uniformly mixed in.

3. Add the fat of your choice (butter, ghee, lard, or tallow yield the best flavor) to the food processor. Process until the dough appears crumbly. Add the remaining tablespoon of water one teaspoon at a time and pulse until the dough starts to form a ball (the humidity in your area can effect how much water is needed).

4. Dump the dough into a 9" round tart or pie pan (or a 5x14," as was used here). Press the dough evenly along the bottom and sides. Move the pan to the refrigerator and chill for 30 minutes.

5. Preheat the oven to 350F.

6. While the dough is chilling, prepare the filling. Crisp up the bacon and crumble it to small pieces. Brown the sausage and the ham and mix them together with the bacon pieces.

7. In a separate large bowl, combine the eggs, coconut milk, scallions, and black pepper. Whisk until fluffy and smooth.

8. Once the dough is chilled, pour the meat into the crust-lined pan. Spread it out evenly. Pour the egg mix in amongst the meat.

9. Move the pan to the oven and bake for 25-30 minutes or until the top is golden and the egg is set in the center. Allow the quiche to cool for at least 10 minutes before cutting and serving (to help keep the crust from crumbling too much).

Note: If using a deep quiche pan (greater than 2" depth), you can double the eggs for more volume.

Yields: 4-6 servings

Meat-Lover's
QUICHE

Mexican Taco
CASSEROLE

> *No need for a tortilla here, this casserole satisfies even the toughest taco cravings.*

THE CASSEROLE

1 lb.	80/20 ground beef
3 c.	butternut squash, *cubed*
1	medium red onion, *chopped*
1	red bell pepper, *chopped*
6 oz.	black olives, *sliced*
4 oz.	roasted green chilies
2	garlic cloves, *minced*
8	eggs
1/2 c.	crushed plantain chips
	chopped tomato, scallions & cilantro (*optional for garnish*)

TACO SEASONING

1 tsp.	sweet paprika
1 tsp.	smoked paprika
1 tsp.	ground cumin
1/2 tsp.	garlic powder
1/2 tsp.	onion powder
1/2 tsp.	dried oregano
1/4 tsp.	cayenne or chipotle powder
1 tsp.	sea salt
1/2 tsp.	black pepper

Directions:

1. Preheat the oven to 375F. Have a large baking dish ready.
2. Mix the taco seasoning together in a large bowl. Add the ground beef. Stir well to mix in the spices.
3. Heat a wide skillet over low heat. Add the seasoned ground beef and sauté until browned, about 10 minutes. Crumble it as it cooks. Remove the beef with a slotted spoon and reserve for later.
4. Add the butternut squash to the pan and sauté until softened, about 5 minutes. Add the red onion and bell pepper and sauté until all the veggies begin to brown, about 5 more minutes.
5. Turn the heat off and add the olives (natural black or green olives are recommended), green chilies, and garlic. Stir well and pour everything into the large baking dish.
6. In a large bowl, whisk the eggs well. Pour them over the casserole ingredients and move everything around to form a fairly even layer.
7. Bake for 30-40 minutes, or until the center is set up (cook times will vary based on the width of your baking dish).
8. While the casserole is cooking, mix together chopped tomatoes, scallions, cilantro and a pinch of sea salt and black pepper for a quick pico de gallo topping, as desired. You can also crumble some plantain chips for a crunchy "Frito casserole" type topping when serving.
9. Allow the casserole to cool for 5-10 minutes before serving. Save leftovers in the refrigerator for up to a week.

> *Yields: 6-8 servings*

TOMATO SAUCE

1	medium onion, *chopped*
3	garlic cloves, *minced*
1/4 c.	white wine (*or lemon juice*)
1 lb.	tomatoes, *chopped*
12 oz.	jarred tomato sauce
1/2 tsp.	sea salt
1/4 tsp.	black pepper
1	bunch parsley, *chopped**
2	sprigs oregano, *chopped*
6	mint leaves, *chopped*
4-8	eggs, *room temperature*

KEFTA MEATBALLS

1 lb.	ground lamb
1 tsp.	ground cumin
1 tsp.	onion powder
1 tsp.	cinnamon
1 tsp.	sweet paprika
1/2 tsp.	ground coriander
1 tsp.	sea salt
1/2 tsp.	black pepper

Directions:

1. Mix the meatball ingredients together gently with a fork. Roll about 20 small meatballs.

2. Heat a large skillet over medium heat and grease lightly with high-heat cooking oil. Cook the meatballs by rolling them into the pan gently and shaking every couple of minutes to keep them rounded and browned on all sides. Be careful not to crowd the pan and cook in batches, as needed. Once browned, remove the meatballs to a plate for later.

3. Add the chopped onion to the hot grease leftover from the meatballs and keep the heat on medium. Sauté until the onion is translucent, about 3-5 minutes. Add the minced garlic and white wine and scrape any browned bits from the bottom of the pan. Add the chopped tomatoes, tomato sauce, sea salt, and black pepper. Bring the sauce to a simmer and reduce the heat to medium low. Simmer until the fresh tomato has broken down, about 10 minutes.

4. Add the chopped parsley, oregano, and mint and stir well. Move the meatballs back to the pan tuck them into the sauce. Create pockets for the number of eggs being used (adjust according to the number of people being served). Crack the eggs into the pan gently. Cover and cook 4-6 minutes for poached easy, 6-8 minutes for poached medium, and 8-10 minutes for poached well. Remove from the heat and serve immediately.

Optional for garnish: extra chopped parsley or a drizzle of good-quality extra virgin olive oil

Moroccan Kefta (also said Kofta) is a traditional Mediterranean meatball filled with rich spices. When tucked into a savory tomato sauce with poached eggs, you have the perfect family-style weekend brunch.

MOROCCAN & POACHED KEFTA EGGS

Sausage Muffins with Whipped
Parsnips, pg. 32

ON THE GO

A selection of bite-sized and handheld breakfast options for carrying in to work or keeping your little ones happy.

SAUSAGE MUFFINS *with Whipped Parsnips*

A meat and potatoes dish without the potatoes. Parsnips whipped with egg and creamy coconut milk make a rich and satisfying topping for Spiced Breakfast Sausage.

1 lb.	parsnips, *peeled & chopped*
2 Tbsp.	butter, ghee, tallow, or coconut oil
2	garlic cloves, *minced*
1 tsp.	sea salt
1/2 tsp.	black pepper
1/8 tsp.	freshly grated nutmeg
3 Tbsp.	canned full-fat coconut milk, *divided*
2	egg yolks
1	egg white, *for glazing*
1 lb.	Spiced Breakfast Sausage *(pg. 44)*
	Homemade Ketchup *(pg. 47)*
	Optional: chives, for garnish

Yields: 12 mini muffins

Directions:

1. Preheat the oven to 375F.
2. Boil the parsnips in a large pot of water for 15-20 minutes, or until fork tender. Drain the water and add the cooked parsnips to a large food processor.
3. Add the butter, minced garlic, sea salt, black pepper, and grated nutmeg to the parsnips. Process until smooth, about 60 seconds.
4. In a small bowl, whisk together 2 tablespoons of coconut milk and the egg yolks until smooth. With the food processor running, slowly drizzle in the egg mix through the top. Continue to process until the parsnips have grown in volume and turned a pale yellow color, about 60 seconds.
5. To pipe the parsnips in swirls, as shown on page 30, scoop the whipped parsnips into a large bag fitted with a star piping tip. Move the bag to the refrigerator while you prep the rest of the muffins. Alternately, you can use a cookie scoop to portion them out. If using a cookie scoop, there's no need to chill the parsnip whip.
6. Portion the sausage between 12 mini muffin cups (or 6-8 regular size muffins). Press the sausage tightly into the holes of the pan and fill to about 3/4 of the way full. Add 1 teaspoon of ketchup on top of each sausage cup and spread evenly.
7. If piping the parsnips, start toward the outer edge and draw a circle as you pipe, moving toward the center to create a peak. If not piping, simply scoop a large cookie scoop's worth on top of each one (try not to exceed the width of the muffin cups).
8. Whisk the egg white together with the last tablespoon of coconut milk. Gently brush a little bit of the mix over the parsnips.
9. Bake for 20-25 minutes, or until the tops of the parsnip whip begins to turn golden and the sausage is cooked through.

Note: for an egg-free option, simply omit the eggs from the parsnips and brush the tops with just the coconut milk before baking. It will be a little less rich but still delicious.

Yields: 2 wraps

THE WRAPS

1/2 c.	filtered water
2 Tbsp.	unflavored grass-fed gelatin
6	eggs
1/2 tsp.	sea salt
1/4 tsp.	black pepper
	crisped bacon
	tomato slices
	fresh spinach
	ripe avocado slices

CREAMY RANCH

1/2 c.	mayonnaise *(homemade, if possible)*
2 Tbsp.	chopped fresh basil
1 Tbsp.	chopped fresh dill
1 Tbsp.	chopped fresh chives
2	garlic cloves, *minced*
1 Tbsp.	red wine vinegar or lemon juice
2-4 Tbsp.	filtered water
	sea salt & black pepper, *to taste*

Eggy, flourless wraps great for filling with anything you like.

Directions:

1. Prepare the Creamy Ranch by mixing all the ingredients together (or blend for a smoother dressing). The amount of water used will determine how thick or runny the dressing is. Set it aside for later.
2. Prepare the wraps: combine the filtered water and gelatin in a small bowl. Set it aside for 3-5 minutes to bloom.
3. Add the eggs to a blender with the sea salt and pepper. Blend until the eggs are light and frothy. Add in the bloomed gelatin and blend on high until smooth, about 30 seconds.
4. Heat a medium skillet (no wider than 9" diameter) over medium low heat. Lightly grease with high-heat cooking oil and pour half the batter into the pan. Cook until the edges start to brown, about 5 minutes. Then cover with a lid to finish cooking the surface, about 3 more minutes. Slide the wrap out onto a plate and let it cool for a couple of minutes. Repeat with the other half of the batter.
5. Assemble the wraps by layering bacon, tomato, spinach, avocado, and Creamy Ranch inside the wrap, as desired.

SOFT DEVILED EGGS
with Gravlax

A unique take on a classic, allowing for the most nutritious way to enjoy your eggs: a fully cooked white and soft, runny yolk. Toppings can be switched up for your favorites but this gravlax is pretty amazing!

Yields: 12 deviled eggs

6	eggs
4 Tbsp.	mayonnaise (*homemade, if possible*)
1 Tbsp.	chopped fresh dill
2 Tbsp.	capers, *chopped*
1	small garlic clove, *minced*
	Honey-Cured Gravlax (*pg. 42*)
	sweet paprika, *for garnish*
	sea salt & black pepper

Directions:

1. Place 1" of water in a medium saucepan. Bring it to a simmer over medium heat. Gently add the eggs (they should all fit along the bottom). Cover and turn the heat to low. Cook for 8 minutes.
2. Move the pan to the sink and run the eggs under cold water for 3 minutes. When they're cool enough to touch, lightly crack each egg against the side of the pan on multiple sides. Let them sit in the water for 10 minutes to give the water time to loosen the shells. If the water starts to feel warm, change it out for new, cold water.
3. While the eggs are cooling, combine the mayonnaise, dill, capers, and garlic in a small bowl. Mix well.
4. Peel the eggs and wipe them clean with a tea towel. Slice them in half and lay them facing open. Top with a dollop of the mayo mix, a bit of Honey-Cured Gravlax, sweet paprika, sea salt, and black pepper, to taste.

Note: this recipe can easily be doubled by using a wider saucepan to fit more eggs. The eggs can also be steamed for just 5-6 minutes for a fully runny yolk when enjoyed in other preparations.

Like mini frittatas, these egg muffins are great to have on hand for a quick breakfast. Filled with sun-dried tomato and basil, they will add a bright flavor to your mornings.

1 c.	sun-dried tomatoes, *chopped*
1/2 c.	fresh basil, *chopped fine*
3	scallions, *chopped*
2	garlic cloves, *minced*
8	eggs
2/3 c.	canned full-fat coconut milk
1 tsp.	sea salt
1/2 tsp.	black pepper
1/8 tsp.	freshly grated nutmeg

Directions:

1. Preheat the oven to 375F. Grease a 12-cup muffin pan.
2. Combine the sun-dried tomatoes, basil, scallions, and garlic in a medium bowl and stir well. Portion the mix into the 12 muffin cups.
3. Whisk together the eggs, coconut milk, sea salt, pepper, and nutmeg in a minimum 4-cup measuring glass (or other bowl with a spout). Fill the muffin cups evenly with the eggs, filling the cups to about 3/4 full.
4. Bake for 20-25 minutes, or until the tops begin to turn golden. Remove from the oven and allow to cool for 10 minutes before running a butter knife around the edges to remove them. Store extras in the fridge for up to a week.

Yields: 12 egg muffins

Sun-Dried Tomato & BASIL EGG MUFFINS

Directions:

1. Preheat the oven to 375F. Have a 12-cup muffin pan ready.
2. Rinse the potatoes under cold water until the water runs clear, about 3 minutes. Drain excess water and dump the potato shreds into a kitchen towel (or a few paper towels) and pat very dry.
3. Place the potatoes in a large bowl and add the avocado oil, sea salt, and black pepper. Stir well until they're completely coated with oil.
4. Portion the potatoes between the muffin cups and press them down to form nest shapes. Bake for 18-20 minutes, or until the edges are browned.
5. While the potatoes are cooking, crisp up the bacon and crumble it.
6. Once the potatoes are browned, add a bit of crumbled bacon to the bottom of each muffin cup. Then add an egg to each cup on top of the bacon. Cook for 10-16 minutes -- 10 minutes for runny yolks and as much as 16 minutes (or so) for hard yolks.

Note: sweet potatoes can be subbed for the russets but there won't be as much browning.

Crispy hash browns make a flavorful little nest for smoky bacon and baked eggs. These guys reheat well for mornings on the go.

1 lb.	russet potatoes, *peeled and shredded**
1/4 c.	avocado oil
1.5 tsp.	sea salt
1 tsp.	black pepper
4	bacon slices
12	eggs
	chives, *for garnish*

Yields: 12 egg nests

Light, flaky, and buttery -- your taste buds will never guess these biscuits are grain-free. You can leave out the bacon and chives for a plain flavor, just up the butter to 1 full cup.

6	bacon slices
2 Tbsp.	unflavored grass-fed gelatin
1/4 c.	filtered water
2 c.	blanched almond flour
1 c.	tapioca flour (starch)
6 Tbsp.	coconut flour
2 tsp.	baking powder
1/2 tsp.	sea salt
1/2 tsp.	black pepper
2 Tbsp.	fresh chives, *chopped*
2 Tbsp.	bacon grease
14 Tbsp.	butter, *cold and cubed small**
2	eggs, *divided*

Directions:

1. Crisp up the bacon and set it aside. Reserve 2 tablespoons of bacon grease.
2. Combine the gelatin and filtered water in a small bowl. Set it aside to bloom for 3-5 minutes.
3. Add the almond flour, tapioca flour, coconut flour, baking powder, sea salt, and black pepper to a large food processor. Process until combined, about 10 seconds. Add the crisped bacon and chopped chives. Process again until the bacon is broken up into small pieces.
4. Add the bacon grease and cubed butter and process until the dough is crumbly. Use caution not to over-mix. Whisk 1 egg and add it to the food processor. Pulse until the dough barely starts to form a ball.
5. Dump the dough out onto a large piece of parchment paper. Gently knead the dough into a ball and flatten it out into a disc. Place a second piece of parchment over top of the dough and roll it out into a roughly shaped rectangle, 1/2" thick.
6. Remove the top piece of parchment and fold the dough in thirds like folding a letter to put in an envelope (using the bottom parchment to lift the dough when folding helps to keep it from breaking). Place the top parchment back and gently roll the dough back into a large rectangle. Repeat folding the dough on itself two more times.
7. On the last fold, leave the dough folded thick. Press down across the top to just barely compress the layers. Press the sides in to smooth them out. The dough should be at least 1" thick but can be as thick as you like.
8. Cut biscuit shapes with a round cutter by pressing straight down (do not twist the cutter or you'll have uneven rising). Gather scraps and repeat the folding process listed above. Place the biscuits on a lined sheet pan and move the pan to the refrigerator to chill for 30 minutes.
9. Preheat the oven to 375F. Whisk the remaining egg with 1 tablespoon of water. Brush it over the tops of the chilled biscuits. Cook for 15-18 minutes, or until the tops are lightly golden.
10. Allow the biscuits to rest for 5 minutes before eating. If using for a sandwich, they should rest 15-20 minutes before adding your favorite fillings.

Note: the water content in butter makes it the perfect fat for light, airy biscuits. Ghee, lard, tallow, or coconut oil can be substituted but the biscuits may not rise as much.

Yields: 12 biscuits

Bacon and Chive
BISCUITS

Honey-Cured Gravlax, pg. 42

ON THE SIDE

Lighter dishes and sides to compliment your breakfast or brunch spread.

Honey-Cured GRAVLAX

Gravlax is salmon that has been cold-cured in salt, sugar, and dill. Home-curing is easy and healthier with the use of raw honey in place of sugar. It pairs well with Soft Deviled Eggs (pg. 35), Savory Zucchini Pancakes (pg. 55), or as-is with a little fresh lemon juice.

1.5 lb.	full side-body salmon filet
1/2 c.	coarse sea salt
3 Tbsp.	chopped fresh dill
2 Tbsp.	lemon zest
1 Tbsp.	coarse black peppercorns
1/2 c.	raw honey

Directions:

1. Prep the salmon by patting it dry and pulling any remaining pin-bones. Remove the skin by cutting against the underside of the skin with a sharp knife (this is optional but will help the salmon to cure more evenly; you can also ask your butcher to do it).

2. To prepare the cure: mix the sea salt, chopped dill, lemon zest, and black peppercorns. Using a mortar & pestle helps to keep everything ground evenly but you can simply mix it in a bowl. Add the raw honey and stir to form a thick paste.

3. Lay a large piece of saran wrap inside a non-reactive dish (glass, china, or stainless steel--something deep that will catch any leaking juices). Spread about half the curing mix onto the saran wrap in a rough shape of the salmon. Then lay the salmon on top and press it down into the mix. Spread the remaining half of the mix on the top side of the salmon, covering as much of the flesh as possible.

4. Wrap the salmon well with the saran wrap, working any air out. Place a second layer of saran wrap around the salmon in the opposite direction and wrap tightly. Place a large dish or pan overtop the salmon with something heavy inside it to weigh it down (cast iron and cans of tuna work well!).

5. Place the stack in the refrigerator for 12 hours. Remove from the fridge and drain any liquid that's accumulated in the pan. Turn the salmon filet over, place the weights back, and refrigerate another 12 hours.

6. Remove the plastic and rinse the salmon well. You know the salmon is done when it feels slightly firm but not hard (too hard means it's cured too long and will be tough). Slice long, thin slices along the length of the filet with a sharp knife. Store extras in the refrigerator for up to a month. It can also be frozen for longer-term storage.

*Note: a fattier salmon like king (Chinook) is highly recommended for a lighter, more flavorful result. Leaner salmon like Coho can be used but will cure much faster, as quick as 8-12 hours total. Additionally, the thinner your salmon filet, the faster it will cure. If it's thinner than 1", check on it after 8 hours.

*Troubleshooting: if you've already rinsed your salmon off and find that it isn't quite done to your liking, sprinkle any areas that seem uncured (they will feel soft and fleshy when pressed) with a bit of fine sea salt. Wrap tightly with new saran wrap and refrigerate for another 4 hours. Repeat as needed until it has reached a fully cured state.

1 lb.	ground pork
2	garlic cloves, *minced*
1	scallion, *chopped*
2 tsp.	ground sage
1 tsp	ground allspice
1 tsp	sweet paprika
1/2 tsp.	ground cinnamon
1/4 tsp	freshly grated nutmeg
1 tsp	sea salt
1 tsp	black pepper
2 tsp.	maple syrup (*optional*)

Yields: 6 large patties

Full of flavorful spices, this sausage will knock the socks off store-bought alternatives. Make sure to use a minimum 15% fat ground pork (85/15) to keep these patties moist.

Directions:

1. Combine all the ingredients in a large bowl. Mix lightly with a fork.
2. With wet hands, divide the meat into 2" balls. Flatten each ball out into a round patty shape, about 1" thick (this thickness will help prevent overcooking). Place the shaped patties on a plate and put the plate in the refrigerator for 15 minutes to let the meat rest.
3. Heat a large skillet over medium-high heat. Lightly grease the pan and add the chilled patties, careful not to crowd the pan. Flip when the edges change from pink to grey. Keep the pan on medium-high to ensure a golden brown crisp on each side.
4. Let the patties rest for 3-5 minutes before serving.

Note: After shaping, the sausages can be laid out on a sheet pan and frozen for later use. Once frozen solid, place them in a plastic freezer bag, remove as much air as possible, and store them in the freezer. Defrost overnight in the refrigerator before cooking.

SPICED BREAKFAST SAUSAGE

FRITTERS

2 lb.	sweet potatoes or jewel yams *(about 2 medium)*
2	eggs, *whisked*
1 tsp.	onion powder
1 tsp.	garlic salt
1/2 tsp.	black pepper
1 Tbsp.	tapioca flour (starch)

GARLIC DILL SAUCE

1/2 c.	canned coconut cream
1 Tbsp.	chopped fresh dill *(or 2 tsp. dried)*
2 tsp.	fresh lemon juice *(or more)*
1	garlic clove, *minced*
pinch	sea salt & black pepper

SWEET POTATO FRITTERS
with Garlic Dill Sauce

These fritters are not fried but still crispy on the outside and moist on the inside. Pair them with a creamy Garlic Dill Sauce or at the bottom of a California Benny stack (pg. 12).

Directions:

1. Peel and shred the sweet potatoes with the shred attachment of a food processor or a box grater. Add them to a large bowl and toss them with a few pinches of sea salt. Allow them to rest in the salt for about 5 minutes to pull some of the moisture out.

2. Run the sweet potatoes under cold water until the water runs clear, about 3 minutes. Pour them into a large tea towel and twist the towel to squeeze as much liquid out as possible.

3. Dump the shredded sweet potato back into the large bowl and add the eggs, onion powder, garlic salt, and black pepper. Stir well until all the shreds are coated with egg. Sprinkle the tapioca flour over top and mix it in well.

4. Heat a large skillet over medium heat. Add a generous amount of high-heat cooking fat (lard or tallow lend great flavor here). Drop the sweet potato into the pan in circle shapes, pressing down on the tops to even them out to about 1/2" thickness. Cook until the edges start to brown, about 3-5 minutes. Flip and cook the second side about 3 more minutes. Move the cooked fritters to a cooling rack to rest for a few minutes before serving.

5. While the fritters are sautéing, prepare the Garlic Dill Sauce by whisking all the ingredients together. Adjust the amount of lemon juice used to achieve the desired consistency.

PLANTAIN TATER TOTS
with Homemade Ketchup

A twist on a familiar childhood favorite, dipped in a savory homemade ketchup

PLANTAIN TATER TOTS

1	large green plantain (~10")
1 Tbsp.	lard, tallow, or avocado oil (*plus more for sautéing*)
	sea salt & black pepper

HOMEMADE KETCHUP

1/2	large white onion, *chopped*
2	garlic cloves, *minced*
12 oz.	tomato paste
3 c.	filtered water
2 Tbsp.	honey
1 Tbsp.	blackstrap molasses
2 Tbsp.	apple cider vinegar
1 tsp.	sweet paprika
2 tsp.	ground mustard
1/4 tsp.	ground allspice
1/4 tsp.	ground cloves
1/2 tsp.	ground cinnamon
1 tsp.	black pepper
2 tsp.	sea salt

Yields: 12 tots

Tater Tots Directions:

1. Roughly chop the plantain. Add it with the lard to the bowl of a large food processor. Process for 10 seconds at a time until the mixture is slightly chunky and sticky. Be careful not to fully puree it or it will be difficult to shape into tots.
2. Heat a skillet over medium heat (cast iron or non-stick is best). Add enough lard to cover the bottom of the pan well.
3. Shape the tots by scooping about a tablespoon of dough with wet hands. Roll it into a ball, then roll long-ways between your hands, and finally squeeze the ends to form a tot shape. It may seem difficult to get a perfect shape with the wet batter but they'll be easier to finish shaping as they cook.
4. Roll the shaped tots into the hot oil. Cook until golden brown on all sides, using a spatula to press them into a tot shape. Work in batches, careful not to crowd the pan. Move the cooked tots onto a paper-towel-lined plate. Season with sea salt and black pepper, as desired.

Notes:
--Only green plantains will work here, not the more ripe yellow or green/yellow-skinned ones.
--Any animal fat will yield the best flavor when pan-frying; coconut oil can be used but it will result in a less savory tater tot, as it can bring out the banana-like flavor.
--This recipe can be made solo but is much easier with two people: one person for shaping the sticky tots dough and one person for pan-frying.

Yields: 1 quart

Ketchup Directions:

1. Heat a large saucepan over medium heat. Add the onion and sauté until translucent, about 3 minutes. Add the garlic and sauté another 60 seconds.
2. Add the remaining ingredients and whisk until smooth. When the sauce begins to simmer, reduce the heat to low and cook for 15-20 minutes or until it has thickened significantly.
3. Pour the ketchup into a blender and blend until smooth, using caution with blending the hot liquid (blending on low speed in two batches is a safe method). If you like your ketchup chunky, you can skip this step. Pour the ketchup into a glass quart jar and store in the refrigerator for up to 2 weeks.

Note: for smaller households, half this recipe can be frozen for later use.

Chorizo & SWEET POTATO HASH

1 lb.	pork chorizo sausage
1	large sweet potato or yam, *peeled and cubed*
1	medium onion, *chopped*
1	red bell pepper, *chopped*
1	green bell pepper, *chopped*
1/2 c.	fresh cilantro, *chopped*
	sea salt & black pepper

> *Both smoky and spicy, this hash is a great side dish for those who can handle some heat in the kitchen! Make sure to choose Mexican chorizo and not the cured Spanish chorizo alternative, which is more like salami than sausage.*

Directions:

1. Heat an extra-large skillet over medium heat. Add the chorizo and cook until browned. Remove the chorizo to a paper towel-lined plate.
2. If the pan is dry, add a bit of high-heat cooking oil. Add the sweet potatoes and cook until softened, about 5 minutes. Add the onion and bell peppers and continue to sauté until everything begins to brown. Stir the chorizo back in along with the chopped cilantro and pour the mix out into a bowl. Season with sea salt and black pepper, as desired.

Yields: 4-6 servings

CRISPY PANCETTA POTATOES

When thinly sliced fingerlings are fried in that extra pancetta grease, you will be in crispy potato heaven. Enjoy as-is, with poached eggs, or dipped in some Herbed Hollandaise (pg. 60).

4 oz.	pancetta, *cubed small*
1/2	white onion, *chopped*
1 lb.	fingerling potatoes, *sliced*
2 Tbsp.	chopped fresh rosemary
1 tsp.	sea salt
pinch	black pepper

Yields: 4-6 servings

Directions:

1. Add the pancetta to a large skillet over medium heat. Cook until browned, about 5 minutes. Remove the pancetta from the pan with a slotted spoon and reserve for later. Leave the grease in the pan.

2. Add the chopped onion to the hot pancetta grease and cook until translucent, about 3 minutes. Add the fingerling potatoes, rosemary, sea salt, and black pepper.

3. Spread the potatoes evenly across the bottom of the pan to encourage browning. Stir every couple of minutes and spread them out again. Repeat until most of the potatoes are browned on the outside and soft on the inside.

4. Add the crisped pancetta back in and serve immediately.

Spicy Salsa Sauerkraut, pg. 52

FRUIT & VEG

Condiments and side dishes designed to help you get a nutrient-dense morning meal.

SPICY SALSA SAUERKRAUT

This recipe is the love child of two of my very favorite condiments: salsa and sauerkraut. Kick up the nutritional value of a great salsa recipe by adding gut-friendly bacteria from fermentation. It is best to read through all the directions before beginning.

1	small head cabbage, *roughly chopped*
4 Tbsp.	good-quality sea salt*
4	medium tomatoes, *roughly chopped*
2	mild peppers**
1	jalapeño (*can half or omit it for less spicy*)
1	large white onion, *roughly chopped*
1	large bunch fresh cilantro
3	garlic cloves
2	limes, *juiced*
2 Tbsp.	raw apple cider vinegar
2 tsp.	dried oregano
1 tsp.	ground cumin

Directions:

1. Place the cabbage in a large food processor. Pulse to break it up into smaller pieces. Pour it out into a large bowl and add the sea salt. Toss to combine and leave it to sit for 10 minutes.
2. After the cabbage has rested 10 minutes, use clean (or gloved) hands to squeeze and mash it. Continue to squeeze until you've pulled quite a bit of liquid out.
3. Add the tomatoes to the food processor. Process until it reaches a consistency you like (both chunky or smooth are ok). Pour it in the bowl with the mashed cabbage.
4. Cut and deseed the peppers and jalapeño. Add them to the food processor with the onion, cilantro, garlic, lime juice, apple cider vinegar, oregano, and cumin. Process until everything is chopped small, stopping to scrape down the sides as needed. Pour the mix in with the tomatoes and cabbage and stir well.
5. With a spoon or wide mouth funnel, portion the salsa into 2 quart-size glass jars. Using a vegetable tamper or large spoon, press the vegetables toward the bottom of the jars. Continue to press until liquid has risen above the vegetables.
6. Cover the jars with coffee filters, cheese cloth, or tea towels secured with rubber bands (you can also use regular canning lids but screw them on loosely to allow gases to escape).
7. Leave the salsa on the counter at 70-80F for 4 days. Each day or two, uncover and press the vegetables down again to releases any gases.
8. After 4 days, taste the salsa. If it still tastes fairly salty, cover it again and let it go another 3-5 days. Temperature and humidity will impact how quickly the salsa ferments; colder temperatures will greatly slow down the process. After making a batch or two, you'll be able to gauge how many days the salsa needs to reach the right level of tanginess in your environment.
9. Once cultured, the salsa will keep in the refrigerator for 3 months or more.

Note on fermenting: the high level of salt is needed to react with the sugars in the vegetables and create the friendly bacteria. When it's ready, most of the salt will no longer be present. You can choose to skip the culturing process by halving of sea salt and skipping the fermenting steps. Seal the salsa and store it in the refrigerator for up to a week. Iodized salt is not recommended for fermenting.

Note on choosing a mild pepper: anaheim, peppadew, cherry bomb, or banana peppers work well.

THE GAZPACHO

1/2 c.	raw almonds, soaked 4+ hours
1	mango, *peeled & cored*
1	small pineapple, *peeled & cored*
1	medium seedless cucumber
1	red, orange, or yellow bell pepper
1/2	medium red onion
1	bunch fresh cilantro
2	garlic cloves
2	limes, *juiced*
1/2 tsp.	sea salt
pinch	black pepper

THE SHRIMP

16	raw shrimp, *peeled & deveined*
	ground smoked paprika
	sea salt & black pepper
	fresh avocado, *for serving*

Tropical Gazpacho
WITH SMOKY SHRIMP

A fresh and flavorful soup with a bit of sweetness from fresh mango and pineapple.

Directions:

1. To make the gazpacho: add the soaked almonds to a large food processor or blender. Pulse until broken up into small pieces.
2. Roughly chop the remaining ingredients and add them in. *For chunky gazpacho*: pulse until it's chopped up small and there's a fair amount of liquid. *For smooth gazpacho*: process or blend on high speed for 30-60 seconds. Set the gazpacho aside for 15 minutes to let the flavors meld while you prepare the shrimp.
3. Season the shrimp generously with smoked paprika, sea salt, and black pepper.
4. Heat a large skillet over medium heat and lightly grease with high-heat cooking oil. Add the shrimp to the hot pan and cook until browned, about 2 minutes per side.
5. Enjoy the gazpacho with the sautéed shrimp and fresh avocado slices, as desired.

Yields: 4 servings

VEGGIE HASH BROWNS

Yields: 12 hash browns

The perfect low-glycemic alternative to your regular potato hash brown. Packed full of onion and herb flavor, they make a great side to any breakfast dish.

2	medium parsnips
1	small yellow squash or zucchini
1	medium carrot
2 tsp.	sea salt
2	scallions, *chopped*
1	garlic clove, *minced*
1/2 c.	fresh basil, *chopped*
1 Tbsp.	fresh rosemary, thyme, or sage, *chopped*
1 Tbsp.	tapioca flour (starch)*
	sea salt & black pepper, *to taste*

Directions:

1. Shred the parsnips, squash, and carrot and place them in a large bowl. Toss in the sea salt and set them aside to rest for 10 minutes.
2. After 10 minutes, run the vegetables under cold water until the water runs clear, about 3 minutes. Dump the vegetables into a large tea towel and wring the towel to squeeze out as much moisture as possible.
3. Once you've gotten most of the water out, dump the dried vegetables back into the bowl. Stir in the scallions, garlic, and herbs. Sprinkle the tapioca flour over top and mix very well to coat all the shreds.
4. Heat a large skillet over medium heat and add some high heat cooking oil. Take a scoop of the vegetables and drop it into the pan. Use a spatula to press the edges in and shape it into a rough circle, about 1/2" thick.
5. Cook until the edges start to brown, pressing the hash brown down occasionally with the back of a spatula. Cook them in batches of 2-3 and be careful not to crowd the pan. Add additional oil if the pan dries up.
6. Carefully flip to cook the other side. A dark golden color is good for flavor but if your patties are getting too charred, turn the heat down just a bit.
7. Remove the cooked patties to a cooling rack. Season with sea salt and black pepper, as desired. For maximum crispiness, enjoy immediately.

*Note: these can be cooked up without the tapioca flour but they will not hold a shape well. Simply spread the shreds out into the pan and toss to brown all sides.

Savory Zucchini PANCAKES

4 c.	shredded zucchini *(about 2 medium)*
2	garlic cloves, *minced*
3	eggs
1/4 c.	canned light coconut milk
2 tsp.	fresh lemon juice
1/4 c.	blanched almond flour
1/4 c.	coconut flour
1 tsp.	onion powder
1/2 tsp.	baking soda
1 tsp.	sea salt
1/2 tsp.	black pepper

Just like your favorite zucchini bread but in the quick-cooking form of a pancake. These cook up light and airy and packed full of nutrients.

Directions:

1. Place the shredded zucchini in a large tea towel. Wring the towel to squeeze out as much moisture as possible (there will be quite a bit). Dump the dried zucchini into a large bowl and add the minced garlic.
2. In a separate bowl, combine the remaining ingredients and whisk well to form a batter. Pour the batter over the zucchini and stir to combine.
3. Heat a large skillet over medium heat. Lightly grease the skillet with high-heat cooking oil and drop batter into the pan in pancake shapes. Smooth the tops down to bring them to a 1/2" thickness. When the edges start to bubble and brown, flip to cook the second side.
4. Move the cooked pancakes to a cooling rack to rest for a couple of minutes before serving.

Yields: 8 pancakes

Sea Vegetable KIMCHI

A traditional fermented Korean dish, Kimchi is a spicy, often fishy take on sauerkraut.

Fish sauce is used here to simplify the process and the addition of seaweed ups both the familiar "umami" factor and nutritional content.

1	small head napa cabbage
4	medium carrots
2	medium daikon radishes
2 Tbsp.	good-quality sea salt*
1/2 c.	dried wakame or dulse seaweed
4	green onions, *chopped*
3	garlic cloves, *minced*
1 Tbsp.	freshly grated ginger
2 tsp.	fish sauce
1-3 Tbsp.	Korean red pepper powder**

Yields: 1 quart

Directions:

1. Shred, slice, or chop the napa cabbage, carrots, and daikon radish. Add them to a large bowl and sprinkle with the sea salt. Toss well to stir in the salt and let the vegetables rest for 10 minutes.
2. While the vegetables are resting in the sea salt, place the dried seaweed in a bowl with enough warm water to fully submerge the seaweed. Leave it to rehydrate for 2-3 minutes.
3. After the vegetables have rested 10 minutes, use clean (or gloved) hands to squeeze and mash the vegetables. Continue to squeeze until you've pulled quite a bit of liquid out of them.
4. Strain the seaweed and add it to the vegetables. Then add the green onions, garlic, ginger, fish sauce, and red pepper. Stir very well until the seaweed is broken up and everything is mixed together.
5. Scoop the kimchi into a glass quart jar fitted with a tight seal (a fido jar is shown here but a regular ball jar would work too).
6. Using a vegetable tamper or a large spoon, press the kimchi down toward the bottom as you scoop it in. It may not seem like it will fit in the jar at first but continue to press it down until everything is in the jar. Press the vegetables so they're submerged below the surface of the liquid.
7. Seal the jar tight and place it in a warm, dark spot in the kitchen. Let stand for 48 hours. After 24 hours, open the jar briefly to allow excess gases to escape. If you can see bubbles appearing throughout the vegetables, you know that the fermentation process is underway.
8. Test the kimchi after the first 48 hours to gauge for flavor. If it's still fairly salty, press the vegetables down again and let it ferment for another 48 hours. Be sure to open the jar daily to release gases. Continue this process until the kimchi has reached a flavor balance you enjoy. It should be slightly salty with a fairly sour or pungent taste.
9. Move the finished kimchi to the refrigerator. It should last 3 months or more (but you'll likely eat it all before that point!).

*Note: iodized salt is not recommended for fermenting.

**Note: Korean red pepper is traditional but any red chili pepper will do, including chili flakes. Use caution with the amount added, as it will increase in spiciness with time. The kimchi shown here had just 2 teaspoons (I'm a wuss) so it's a lighter red color than it would be with a traditional amount of red pepper. Whatever level of heat you can handle, it will still be delicious.

Peach and Prosciutto Slaw

This salad is best enjoyed after the dressing has had a chance to soften the vegetables for about 30 minutes. It stays crisp and the flavors only get better with time, making it a great prepare-ahead side dish.

THE DRESSING

2 Tbsp.	lemon juice
1 Tbsp.	apple cider vinegar
1 Tbsp.	raw honey
1 tsp.	freshly grated ginger
3 Tbsp.	mayonnaise (homemade, if possible)
1/2 tsp.	sea salt
1/4 tsp.	black pepper

THE SLAW

1/2	small head napa cabbage
1	fennel bulb (with fronds)
1	medium celery root, peeled
2	carrots, julienned
6	small mint leaves, minced
1/2 c.	chopped basil
3 oz.	prosciutto
2	peaches or nectarines, sliced

DIRECTIONS

1. Prepare the dressing by combining all the ingredients in a small bowl. Whisk well until it's smooth and set it aside for later.
2. Shred the napa cabbage, fennel, and celery root with the shredding attachment of a food processor (or thinly slice with a knife). Toss them together in a large bowl with the julienned carrots, mint, and basil. Tear the prosciutto into thin strips and add them to the bowl along with the sliced peaches.
3. Pour the dressing over top of the slaw and stir well.

HERBED HOLLANDAISE & BROCCOLINI

This eggy sauce will make any veggie taste like breakfast. It works just as well without the garlic and herbs but I have yet to find an occasion to leave them out.

6 Tbsp.	butter, ghee, or extra virgin olive oil*
2	fresh egg yolks**
3 Tbsp.	lemon juice
1	garlic clove, *chopped*
10	fresh chives, *chopped*
1/2 tsp.	black pepper
2-4 Tbsp.	warm water
1 lb.	broccolini, *steamed*

Directions:

1. Melt the butter over low heat (do not boil). Cover to keep it warm.
2. Add the egg yolks, lemon juice, garlic, chives, and black pepper to a blender. Blend on high until smooth, about 20 seconds.
3. . With the blender on the lowest speed, drizzle the warm butter in through the top. Turn the speed to high and blend for no more than 8-10 seconds.
4. Scrape down the sides and check the thickness of the sauce. If desired, add 2-4 tablespoons of warm water to thin it out to your desired consistency. Add it 1 tablespoon at a time and pulse the blender to incorporate.
5. Serve the sauce over steamed broccolini. If not serving immediately, it may thicken or separate. Simply add one tablespoon of hot water and pulse the blender to smooth out the sauce before serving.

Note: butter or ghee will yield a more traditional hollandaise flavor. If using unsalted butter, ghee or extra-virgin olive oil, add a pinch of sea salt to the sauce.

**Note: although the fat added is warmed, it will not be hot enough to fully cook the egg yolks. Therefore, it's best if fresh, pastured egg yolks are used.*

2	bacon slices
1	shallot, *minced*
1/2 lb.	brussels sprouts, *shaved**
1/2 lb.	asparagus, *chopped*
1	medium green apple, *chopped*
3	swiss chard leaves, *chopped*
3	kale leaves, *chopped*
1	garlic clove, *minced*
1/2	lemon, *juiced*
1/4 c.	toasted pine nuts

WARM GREENS WITH
Bacon and Apple

Bacon, tart green apple, bright lemon juice, and toasty pine nuts lift the best flavors out of thick, leafy greens. And for those in need of a little less whining at the table over vegetables, this dish is a great place to hide those brussels sprouts.

Directions:

1. Heat a large skillet over medium heat. Cook the bacon until crisp and remove it to a paper towel. Once cooled, crumble the bacon into small pieces. Leave the bacon grease in the pan for cooking the greens.
2. Turn the heat to medium low and add the minced shallot. Sauté until softened, about 3 minutes. Add the brussels sprouts, asparagus, and green apple. Cook until the brussels sprouts and apple are soft, about 5 minutes.
3. Add the chard, kale, and garlic and sauté until the leaves have barely started to wilt. Turn the heat off and stir in the lemon juice. Toss with the crisped bacon and toasted pine nuts.

Note: a mandoline is perfect for shaving brussels sprouts thin but a very sharp knife will work, as well.

Yields: 4 servings

Cranberry Apple STUFFED SQUASH

Not just for the winter months, this earthy side dish will bring on warm and cozy mornings when you need them most.

1	acorn squash
1 c.	assorted nuts, *soaked 2+ hours**
1/4 c.	unsweetened dried cranberries
6	fresh sage leaves
2 Tbsp.	butter, ghee, or coconut oil
pinch	sea salt
1	medium apple, *roughly chopped*
	honey, *for serving (optional)*

Yields: 4 servings

Directions:

1. Preheat the oven to 375F.
2. Cut the squash in half and remove the seeds. Lay the squash facing open on a lined baking sheet.
3. Add the nuts, cranberries, sage leaves, butter, and sea salt to the bowl of a food processor. Pulse a few times to roughly chop everything together. Add the apple and pulse again to incorporate, being carefully not to over-process or the mix will get soggy.
4. Portion the blended fruit and nuts into the two halves of squash. Fill the cavities and use your hands to make a small heap on each of the squash, as needed.
5. Cover the squash loosely with tinfoil and bake for 30 minutes. Remove the foil and bake for another 15 minutes, or until the tops are golden brown and the squash pierces easily with a fork.
6. Drizzle with honey to serve, as desired.

*Note: any nuts work, so use whatever you prefer. Pecans and almonds are pictured here.

Strawberries and Cream
Crepes, pg. 66

SWEET STARTS

For those mornings when you need a little something special.

Crisp edges and a soft, buttery texture -- these crepes are the real deal. Great for both sweet and savory fillings or enjoyed as-is with a squirt of lemon juice.

1/2 c.	canned light coconut milk
1/2 c.	filtered water
2	eggs
2 Tbsp.	melted butter, ghee, or coconut oil (*plus more for greasing*)*
2 tsp.	vanilla extract
1 Tbsp.	honey (*optional*)
pinch	sea salt
1/4 c.	tapioca flour (starch)
3 Tbsp.	coconut flour
	fresh strawberries
	plain whipped coconut cream
	any other toppings your heart desires

Directions:

1. Combine the coconut milk, water, eggs, butter, vanilla, honey (if using), and sea salt in a blender. Blend on high until smooth. Add the tapioca flour and coconut flour and blend again. Let the batter rest 3 minutes to allow the coconut flour to absorb liquid and blend again until smooth. Keep the batter in the blender for easy pouring when cooking the crepes.

2. Heat a large skillet over medium-low heat for cast iron or medium heat for nonstick pans. Once hot, add a bit of butter and a small amount of batter (the amount of batter per crepe will differ depending on the size of your pan). Quickly tip the pan to spread the batter evenly across the bottom. It should be thin enough to see the bottom of the pan through the bubbles.

3. Cook until the edges of the crepe start to brown, rotating the pan over the heat to brown evenly as needed. Use a thin spatula to gently lift one side up, slide the spatula further underneath and flip the crepe over (this might take practice with 1-2 crepes). Cook until it lifts easily from the pan, another 60 seconds or so. Slide the finished crepes onto a plate and cover with a tea towel to keep them warm and pliable. Repeat with the remaining batter.

4. Fill with fresh strawberries, whipped coconut cream, your favorite melted dark chocolate bar, and chopped nuts, as desired.

Note: butter and ghee add a more familiar "crepe" flavor to this recipe but coconut oil can be used for dairy-free. Up the sea salt to 1/4 tsp. if using coconut oil.

STRAWBERRIES & CREAM CREPES

Yields: 8 large crepes

3.5 oz.	frozen acai puree *(unsweetened)*
1/2	large orange, *peeled*
1/2	medium lemon, *peel included*
1 c.	frozen berries *(any)*
2 Tbsp.	red palm oil*
1/2 - 1 c.	pomegranate juice, cranberry juice, or coconut water
	For Topping:
	banana or other fruit slices
	nuts or seeds
	coconut flakes or "granola"

Yields: 1-2 bowls

ACAI BREAKFAST BOWL

This bowl is packed with antioxidant-rich ingredients, making it the perfect indulgence. Frozen acai puree packs can be found in most health food stores.

Directions:

1. Soften the acai puree in warm water for 2-3 minutes, or until it's easy to break apart. Chop the orange and lemon and add them to a blender with the softened acai, frozen berries, and red palm oil.

2. Add 1/2 cup of your liquid of choice (pomegranate juice is a personal favorite). Blend on low speed for 30 seconds. If the blender gets stuck, add small amounts of liquid until it blends smoothly. This bowl is best enjoyed with a thick, sorbet-like puree. Blending too long or adding too much liquid will yield a more smoothie-like consistency. Scraping down the sides helps to ensure the red palm oil is mixed in thoroughly.

3. Pour into a bowl and garnish with your favorite fresh toppings.

*Note: red palm oil is a saturated fat that's very high in carotenes, a type of antioxidant. It lends a delicious, light carrot taste and a creamy texture to this puree.

One of my favorite breakfasts as a child. A pancake (of sorts) that puffs up enormously in the oven. The result is a light, airy, and eggy dish that melts in your mouth. While still warm, top with a fresh butter packed with spices and roasted apple.

GERMAN PANCAKES

6	eggs
1/2 c.	canned light coconut milk
4 Tbsp.	melted butter, ghee, or coconut oil (*divided*)
2 Tbsp.	honey or maple syrup (*optional*)
2 tsp.	vanilla extract
3/4 c.	blanched almond flour
3 T.	tapioca flour (starch)
1/8 tsp.	freshly ground nutmeg
pinch	sea salt

ROASTED APPLE BUTTER

2	large apples, *cubed small*
1/2 c.	butter or ghee, *softened*
1 Tbsp.	coconut palm sugar (*optional*)
1 Tbsp.	ground cinnamon
1 tsp.	ground ginger

Directions:

1. To make the Apple Butter: place the cubed apple on a lined baking sheet. Cook at 400F until browned, about 40 minutes, tossing the apples midway through. Allow them to cool to room temperature.
2. Add the softened butter, coconut sugar, cinnamon, and ground ginger to a stand mixer fitted with the whisk attachment. Beat on medium high until whipped and fluffy. Add the cooled apples and beat again to incorporate. Keep at room temperature until serving; store extras in the refrigerator for up to a week.
3. To make the German Pancakes: turn the oven down to 350F. Place a 9" cast iron or stone dish into the oven with 2 tablespoons of butter.
4. Combine all the ingredients in a blender in the order listed so liquids are at the bottom. Blend on high until smooth, about 60 seconds.
5. When the pan in the oven is hot and the butter begins to bubble and brown, carefully pour the pancake batter into the pan. Close the oven door and cook for 25-30 minutes, or until it has puffed up and the top is lightly golden.

GERMAN PANCAKES WITH
Roasted Apple Butter

Chocolate Chip BANANA PANCAKES

2	very ripe bananas
2	eggs
1/4 c.	canned light coconut milk
2 tsp.	vanilla extract
3 Tbsp.	melted butter, ghee, or coconut oil *(plus more for cooking)*
3/4 c.	blanched almond flour
2 Tbsp.	coconut flour
1/2 tsp.	sea salt
1/2 tsp.	baking powder
1/4 tsp.	baking soda
	dark chocolate chips

Mini chocolate chips have a place in any pancake but particularly those sweetened with ripe bananas. This recipe is approved for all ages.

Directions:

1. Add the bananas, eggs, coconut milk, vanilla, and butter to a blender. Blend until smooth. Add the almond flour, coconut flour, sea salt, baking powder, and baking soda. Blend again until smooth. Let the batter rest 2-3 minutes to let the coconut flour absorb more moisture and blend once more.

2. Heat a wide skillet over medium low heat. Add a bit of butter to the pan and pour the batter to form pancakes. Use the back of a spoon to smooth each pancake to about 1/4" thickness. Sprinkle a handful of chocolate chips onto each pancake.

3. When the pancakes begin to rise and form a few bubbles on the surface, flip them over (about 3-4 minutes). Cook until just set on the second side, about 2 minutes more. Move them to a cookie sheet until serving.

4. Top with additional bananas, chocolate chips, butter, or maple syrup, as desired.

1/2 c.	butter or ghee
4	eggs
1/2 c.	canned light coconut milk
1/3 c.	maple syrup
1 Tbsp.	blackstrap molasses
2 Tbsp.	vanilla extract
1 tsp.	sea salt
1 tsp.	apple cider vinegar
2 c.	blanched almond flour
1 c.	tapioca flour (starch)
1 tsp.	baking powder
1/2 tsp.	baking soda

Browned butter (or ghee) takes waffles to a whole new level. You can use coconut oil here but the flavors will be slightly different. Top with more browned butter and maple syrup to enhance the caramelized goodness.

Directions:

1. Place the butter in a small saucepan over medium heat. Cook until it bubbles and begins to brown, about 3-5 minutes. Remove it from the heat to let it cool.
2. Add the remaining ingredients to a blender in the order listed (so the liquids are at the bottom). Blend on medium speed until smooth. Add the browned butter and blend again on high for another 15 seconds.
3. Heat your waffle iron to medium (if it has heat controls). If not using a ceramic or non-stick waffle iron, make sure to grease it first. Pour enough batter to fill the holes and cook until golden brown. This may take a few minutes past the "ready" light. They crisp up best when cooked to a warm golden color.
4. Move the cooked waffles to a cooling rack to rest for 2-3 minutes before serving. This allows the steam to escape and the waffles to stay crisp.

Note: don't skip the molasses, as it helps to give these waffles a nice golden color.

Yields: 6 large waffles

Browned Butter WAFFLES

Spiced Pecan COFFEE CAKE

A Christmas morning favorite in my home growing up. I set out to replicate the streusel coffee cake of my youth as closely as possible. The result is a light and airy cake layered with spiced, sweet pecans. This recipe might be your new family favorite.

THE STREUSEL

1 c.	pecans, *soaked 2 hours*
4 Tbsp.	coconut, date, or muscovado sugar
2 Tbsp.	butter, ghee, or coconut oil
1 Tbsp.	ground cinnamon
2 tsp.	ground ginger
1/4 tsp.	ground cloves

THE CAKE

1/2 c.	canned light coconut milk
2 Tbsp	fresh lemon juice
3	eggs
6 Tbsp.	melted butter, ghee, or coconut oil
3 Tbsp.	honey or maple syrup
1 Tbsp.	vanilla extract
1/2 tsp.	sea salt
1 tsp.	baking powder
1/2 tsp.	baking soda
2 1/2 c.	blanched almond flour
1 c.	tapioca flour (starch)

Directions:

1. Preheat the oven to 325F. Grease a 9x9" baking pan.
2. To make The Streusel: add the pecans, coconut sugar, butter, cinnamon, ginger, and cloves to the bowl of a food processor. Process until the mixture is crumbly with no large chunks. Set it aside for later.
3. To make The Cake batter: combine the coconut milk and lemon juice in a small bowl. Set it aside until it starts to curdle a bit (similar to buttermilk), about 3 minutes.
4. Add the eggs, melted butter, honey, vanilla, and sea salt to the bowl of a stand mixer fitted with the paddle attachment. Mix on medium speed until pale and fluffy. Add the curdled coconut milk and mix again.
5. In a separate bowl, whisk together the baking powder, baking soda, almond flour, and tapioca flour. Add the dry mix to the wet ingredients and mix on medium speed until the batter is fairly smooth.
6. Pour half the batter into the greased baking pan. Sprinkle half of the streusel over top of the batter. Pour the remaining half of the batter over the streusel and spread it to cover the streusel as much as possible. Sprinkle the remaining half of the streusel over top the batter.
7. Bake the cake for 30-35 minutes, or until the top is golden and a toothpick inserted into the center comes out clean. Allow the cake to cool for 10 minutes before serving. Top with melted Glaze (pg. 74), as desired.

PROTEIN COOKIES

1/2 c.	plain almond butter
±10	medjool dates
4 Tbsp.	grass-fed collagen peptides *(AKA hydrolysate gelatin)*
1 Tbsp.	virgin coconut oil
1 tsp.	vanilla extract
2 tsp.	ground cinnamon
pinch	ground cloves
1/2 tsp.	sea salt
1 Tbsp.	filtered water
1/2 c.	sliced almonds
1/2 c.	unsweetened shredded coconut
1/4 c.	hulled hemp seeds

THE GLAZE

1/3 c.	coconut butter, *warmed*
1 tsp.	melted butter, ghee, or coconut oil
pinch	vanilla bean powder *(or 1 tsp. extract)*

These sweet, nutty "no-bakes" make a great carbohydrate source for your breakfast or can function as a pre/post-workout snack.

Directions:

1. Combine the almond butter, dates (adjust to desired sweetness), collagen peptides, coconut oil, vanilla, cinnamon, cloves, and sea salt in a large food processor. Pulse until broken up and crumbly.

2. Add the water one teaspoon at a time until the mix becomes sticky (it should stay together when pinched between two fingers). Add in the almonds, coconut, and hemp seeds. Pulse 3-5 times to gently incorporate but leave them a bit chunky.

3. Using a small cookie scoop, portion out the cookies onto a lined cookie sheet. Press them down with the back of the scoop to level out the tops.

4. To make the glaze, whisk the ingredients together until smooth. Drizzling over the cookies works best if the coconut butter is warm but not hot.

5. Drizzle the cookies with the glaze, as desired. Move the pan to the refrigerator for 15 minutes, or until they've hardened slightly. Best kept refrigerated and removed 5 minutes prior to serving.

Note: for a nut-free version, substitute sunflower seed butter for the almond butter and sunflower seeds for the sliced almonds.

Yields: 24 cookies

Cinnamon Roll
PROTEIN COOKIES

These are the muffins of your grain-free dreams!
Moist and fluffy with a sticky cherry sauce through the middle.
They are perfect straight out of the oven or made even more
indulgent with a little pat of butter melted over top.

CHERRY SAUCE

8 oz.	frozen cherries*
1 Tbsp.	fresh lemon juice
1 Tbsp.	honey
2 tsp.	tapioca flour (starch)

THE MUFFINS

1/3 c.	canned light coconut milk
2 Tbsp	fresh lemon juice
3	eggs
6 Tbsp.	melted butter, ghee, or coconut oil
1/4 c.	honey
1 Tbsp.	almond extract
2 tsp.	vanilla extract
1/2 tsp.	sea salt
1 tsp.	baking powder
1/2 tsp.	baking soda
2 1/2 c.	blanched almond flour
1 c.	tapioca flour (starch)

Directions:

1. Make the Cherry Sauce by combining the cherries, lemon juice, honey, and tapioca flour in a medium saucepan. Stir well before turning on the heat.

2. Turn the heat to medium low and stir continuously until the mixture thickens and the cherries begin to break apart. Remove from the heat and set aside for later.

3. Preheat the oven to 325F. Fill a muffin pan with muffin cup liners.

4. To make the muffins: combine the coconut milk and lemon juice in a small bowl. Set it aside until it starts to curdle a bit (similar to buttermilk), about 3 minutes.

5. Add the eggs, melted butter, honey, almond extract, vanilla extract, and sea salt to the bowl of a stand mixer fitted with the paddle attachment. Mix on medium speed until pale and fluffy, about 60 seconds. Add the curdled coconut milk and mix again.

6. In a separate bowl, whisk together the baking powder, baking soda, almond flour, and tapioca flour. Add the dry mix to the wet ingredients and mix on medium speed until the batter is fairly smooth.

7. Portion half of the batter between the 12 muffin cups, filling to about halfway full. Spoon the cherry sauce over top of the batter, about 2 tablespoons per muffin. Portion the remaining batter on top of the cherry sauce.

8. Bake for 20-25 minutes, or until a toothpick comes out clean. The muffins may bubble over just a bit. Allow them to cool in the pan for 10 minutes before removing.

Note: I have tried these muffins with a variety of frozen berries and they all work well. If using a more tart one like raspberries, you may want to up the amount of honey in the sauce.

Yields: 12 muffins

Dark Chocolate HAZELNUT GRANOLA

> *Decadent, yet guilt-free, this rich chocolate granola is mildly sweet and full of nutrients: fiber from the tigernuts (which are not actually nuts), protein from the hazelnuts and almonds, and antioxidant power from raw cacao nibs. Tigernuts are a starchy tuber and can be found easily online. They give this oat-free granola the chewy bite it would otherwise be missing.*

3 Tbsp.	butter, ghee, or coconut oil
3 Tbsp.	maple syrup
1/4 c.	cacao powder
1 Tbsp.	vanilla extract
1/2 tsp.	sea salt
1 c.	tigernuts, *soaked 24 hours**
1 c.	hazelnuts, *soaked 4 hours*
1/2 c.	pumpkin or sunflower seeds
1/2 c.	sliced almonds
1/2 c.	raw cacao nibs

Directions:

1. Preheat the oven to 325F. Line a baking sheet with parchment paper.
2. Combine the butter, maple syrup, cacao powder, vanilla, and sea salt in a small saucepan. Cook over low heat until melted.
3. Place the soaked tigernuts in a large food processor. Process until chopped small. Add the hazelnuts, pumpkin or sunflower seeds, and sliced almonds. Process again until the mix is crumbly. Pour in the melted chocolate mixture and pulse until everything is coated with chocolate.
4. Dump the granola onto the lined baking sheet and spread it out evenly. Bake for 1 hour, removing the pan halfway through to toss the granola.
5. Allow the granola to cool for 15 minutes before breaking it up into pieces and tossing in the raw cacao nibs. Best stored at room temperature.

*Note: if you don't have tigernuts, you can replace them with any nut you like. You can also make this nut-free by replacing all the nuts with tigernuts.

> Yields: about 4 cups granola

Good Morning Tonic, pg 82

DRINKS

For a light start to the day or a warm sip next to your morning meal, there is a little something for everyone here.

Good Morning TONIC

Directions:

1. Place all the ingredients into a magic bullet, spice grinder, or small food processor and blend on high speed for 30-60 seconds, or until smooth.
2. Combine two small spoonfuls with 8 oz. warm water. Best enjoyed in the morning on an empty stomach.
3. Store extra in the fridge and enjoy within 3-4 days for maximum benefit.

Note: ground ginger and turmeric can be used in place of the fresh roots (sub 2 teaspoons each), but I've found the flavor is much more enjoyable with fresh.

Yields: 4 servings

1	large lemon, *juiced & zested*
2 Tbsp.	freshly grated ginger
2 Tbsp.	freshly grated turmeric
1 tsp.	ground cinnamon
tiny pinch	cayenne pepper *(optional)*
1 Tbsp.	raw honey
1 tsp.	sea salt

Lemon: *increases stomach acid to aid digestion; has anti-inflammatory alkalizing effects*

Ginger: *stimulates enzyme secretion to aid digestion; potent antibacterial and anti-fungal properties*

Turmeric: *powerful anti-inflammatory effects to fight chronic illness; both preventative and anti-cancer effects*

Cinnamon: *high levels of anti-oxidants to combat damage from free radicals; curbs sugar cravings and slows the breakdown of carbohydrates into the bloodstream*

Cayenne Pepper: *stimulates the digestive track; increases saliva to better break down foods; boosts the lymphatic system to improve elimination*

Raw Honey: *full of dozens of vitamins, minerals, and live enzymes; promotes the growth of good bacteria in the intestines; counters pollen allergies*

Sea Salt: *contains numerous trace minerals that are difficult to get through diet otherwise, these minerals help to improve hormone function and balance; contains electrolytes like magnesium to ease achy muscles*

Chock full of healthy, filling fats and a matcha-shaped kick in the pants, this smoothie will get your morning going!

1/2 c.	canned light coconut milk
1/4 c.	filtered water
1 Tbsp.	matcha green tea powder
1	ripe banana
1/2	ripe avocado
3 c.	spinach or kale
1/2 tsp.	vanilla bean powder *(or 1 tsp. extract)*
1 Tbsp.	raw honey *(optional)*
1/2 tsp.	sea salt
1-2 c.	ice cubes
2 Tbsp.	grass-fed collagen peptides (hydrolysate gelatin) or whey protein, *optional for added protein*

Directions:

1. Place all the ingredients into a blender and blend on high speed for 30-60 seconds, or until smooth.

Note: if using a very ripe banana, you shouldn't need to add any honey.

Yields: 2 servings

MATCHA AVOCADO SMOOTHIE

Mint and Lime GINGER BEER

An old-school approach to soda making: ginger beer is not actually beer, but a fizzy probiotic-rich drink. Once you have your starter "Bug," you can use it continually to make soda. Cane sugar is required for the fermentation process but you can use muscovado, a dark molasses-rich sugar, for a greater nutritional content. Sugar feeds the ferment and most of it is not present by the time you drink it!

GINGER BUG

1/4+ c.	filtered water
3+ Tbsp.	organic freshly grated ginger
3+ Tbsp.	organic muscovado or organic cane sugar

MINT & LIME SODA

6	mint leaves, *chopped*
1/4 c.	fresh lime juice
3 c.	filtered water
1/2 c.	Ginger Bug liquid

Yields: 1+ quarts

Directions:

Note: this is a 7-10 day process so plan accordingly.

1. *Day 1:* Place 1/4 cup filtered water, 3 tablespoons of grated ginger, and 3 tablespoons of sugar into a large glass jar. Stir with a clean spoon to dissolve most of the sugar. Cover with a coffee filter or tea towel secured with a rubber band. Place it in a warm spot (75-80F) in the kitchen away from direct sunlight.

2. *Days 2-5:* Add another 2 tablespoons of water, 1 tablespoon of ginger, and 1 tablespoon of sugar. Stir well. Repeat this each day through Day 5.

3. *Day 6:* The ginger bug should've started to fizz when stirred on Day 3 or 4. If your bug still isn't fizzing by Day 5, you'll have to toss the batch and start over. Temperature, humidity, and even a dirty spoon can cause it to die or not activate at all. If your bug is fizzing, get the soda ingredients ready for bottling.

4. *To make The Mint & Lime Soda:* add the mint leaves, lime juice, and filtered water to a large measuring glass with a spout. Strain the ginger bug. Pour 1/2 cup of the liquid with the mint/lime water and the rest back into your Ginger Bug jar. For a stronger ginger flavor in your soda, you can add a teaspoon of the ginger bug bits to the soda. Discard the rest of the strained ginger.

5. Portion the soda between glass jars (choose something that has a tight seal like the flip top bottle pictured here). Seal the sodas and leave them on the counter in a warm spot for 2-5 days to get fizzy (if you don't seal them tight, they won't get fizzy). Check them every 24 hours to "burp" the built up CO_2 gas and prevent the bottle from exploding from pressure. If the drink doesn't seem fizzy enough after 2 days, let it go for another 2-3 days. The longer the drink sits, the more sugar will be used up and the less sweet it will be.

6. After making the soda, revive your Ginger Bug by adding the Step #2 ingredients to the reserved liquid. Continue to feed it daily until another 1/2 cup of liquid has accumulated. Repeat Steps #4-5 to make new soda batches with whatever fresh fruit, herbs, or spices that you like. Use the base ratio of 3 cups water to 1/2 cup Ginger Bug Liquid before adding flavors.

MACA SUPER SMOOTHIE

Creamy without any added cream, this rich smoothie relies on the power of egg yolks for a smooth consistency. Though high in calories, it is packed with a diverse array of nutrients and will keep you full for hours.

	Yields: 2 servings
1 c.	filtered water
1/2 c.	almonds, *soaked 4+ hours**
6-8	medjool dates, *adjust for sweetness*
2	fresh egg yolks**
2 Tbsp.	MCT or coconut oil
2 tsp.	raw maca powder
1 Tbsp.	raw cacao nibs
3 Tbsp.	hulled hemp seeds
2 tsp.	vanilla extract
2 tsp.	ground cinnamon
pinch	sea salt
1-2 c.	ice cubes

Directions:

1. Place all the ingredients into a blender and blend on high speed for 30-60 seconds, or until smooth.
2. Stir in extra chopped almonds, cacao nibs, and hemp seeds for a little crunch.

Note: you can substitute 1/4 c. almond butter for the soaked almonds.

**Note: use the freshest, pastured eggs you can get your hands on, as they are not being cooked.*

Yields: 2 cups juice	
1/2	small lemon, *peel included*
	sea salt & black pepper
3	large tomatoes
1	red beet
2	carrots
2	celery stalks
2 c.	spinach, kale, or chard
1/2 c.	fresh parsley
1	garlic clove
2"	fresh horseradish, *peeled*
1/4	small jalapeño *(optional)*
	natural hot sauce or Worcestershire, *for serving*

Directions:

1. Rim a glass with juice from the lemon. Dip into sea salt and black pepper, as desired.
2. Clean and chop all the vegetables and press them through a juicer. (Alternatively, you can blend the ingredients and strain the juice through a fine sieve.)
3. Garnish with hot sauce or Worcestershire, as desired.

Note: adding a little vodka to this makes for a perfect Bloody Mary.

Zesty Garlic
TOMATO JUICE

I was one of those kids who loved canned tomato juice. This recipe is the closest I have come to replicating it homemade. Zesty with just a little bite to it, the flavors are complex and delicious.

The best of both worlds when it comes to warm, comforting drinks: a chai spice blend mixed with a golden turmeric latte. The flavors are robust and satisfying and it makes for a unique alternative to your normal morning brew.

3 c.	filtered water
2" knob	fresh ginger
4" knob	fresh turmeric
10	cardamom pods
1	vanilla bean
10	whole cloves
1	cinnamon stick
1/4 tsp.	freshly grated nutmeg
5	whole black peppercorns
3	whole star anise
4	medjool dates (*optional*)
3 Tbsp.	butter, ghee, red palm oil, coconut oil, and/or MCT oil
2 Tbsp.	unflavored grass-fed gelatin
pinch	sea salt

Directions:

1. Pour the filtered water into a saucepan over medium heat.
2. Smash the ginger, turmeric and cardamom pods with the flat side of a large knife. Split the vanilla bean lengthwise and scrape the seeds out.
3. Add all the smashed bits, cardamom pods and seeds, and vanilla bean and seeds to the saucepan. Then add the cloves, cinnamon stick, grated nutmeg, black peppercorns, and star anise.
4. Bring the water to a simmer, reduce the heat to low, and cover with a lid. Cook for 30-45 minutes, or until the water is fragrant and yellow.
5. Strain all the bits out and pour the spiced water into a blender. Add the dates, fats of your choice (I prefer a combo of red palm and MCT), gelatin, and sea salt. Blend on high until smooth and creamy.

Notes:
* *Ground ginger and turmeric will work in place of the fresh roots but I've found that fresh gives a subtler, more pleasing taste. To substitute, use 2 teaspoons of each in dried form.*
* *2 tablespoons of honey or maple syrup can be used in place of the dates or you can forgo sweetening altogether.*
* *When steeping the spices in the water, you can make this more traditional by adding your favorite black tea in the last 10 minutes of simmering.*

Yields: 2-4 servings

SPICED GOLDEN MILK

CREAMY SPANISH *Horchata*

Directions:

1. Add the tigernuts and the filtered water to a large stock pot. Bring to a boil and reduce the heat to low. Cover and cook for 15 minutes. Remove the lid and simmer uncovered for another 15 minutes.

2. Pour the water and tigernuts into a high-powered blender (a regular blender may not be able to break up the tigernuts enough for a smooth horchata). The water and tigernuts together should come to 4 cups at this point. Add or remove water, as needed. Blend on high speed for 2-3 minutes, or until the horchata is fairly smooth.

3. Line a colander with a tea towel or cheesecloth. Set the lined colander inside a large bowl. Pour the horchata into the tea towel to strain out the tigernut bits. Stirring it helps to move most of the liquid through the tea towel and into the bowl. The tea towel may need to be twisted and wrung out to get the last of the liquid. Use caution, as it will still be very warm.

4. For a more traditional take, you can choose not to strain it and drink it with the coarse bits. Tigernuts are a great source of fiber so this is also a more healthful way to enjoy this drink.

5. Stir the vanilla extract, sea salt, and maple syrup into the horchata. Serve warm with a sprinkle of cinnamon.

Note: to make a raw preparation of this for Raw Tigernut Milk, soak the tigernuts for 48 hours. Skip the boiling and add them directly to the blender with 4 cups of water. Then continue with the steps as listed.

Yields: 4 cups horchata

1 c.	tigernuts, *soaked 24 hours**
6+ c.	filtered water
2 tsp.	vanilla extract
1 tsp.	sea salt
2 Tbsp.	maple syrup
	cinnamon, *for serving*

Tigernuts, AKA chufa, have been used for horchata in Spain for years. They are not actually nuts, but a starchy tuber with a fair amount of fiber that makes this drink thick and creamy.

Sunrise JUICE

Though it looks a lot like OJ, this vibrant juice carries a much lower glycemic load than juiced oranges. Fresh pressed juices can be a great way for those who may not do well on a high-fiber diet to get additional nutrients from fresh vegetables.

1	yam
3	carrots
2	golden beets
1/2	lemon, *peel included*
1	yellow or orange bell pepper
1	grapefruit, *peeled*
1/2 - 1 c.	coconut water
	grass-fed collagen peptides (hydrolysate gelatin), *optional for added protein*

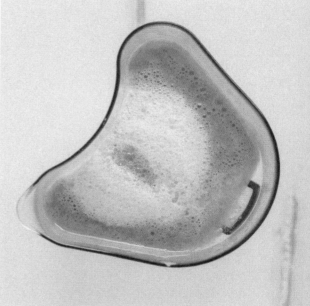

Directions:

1. Chop all the vegetables and press through a juicer.
2. Stir in coconut water and collagen peptides, as desired.

Note: this juice recipe does not do well with blending and straining, as mentioned in the Zesty Garlic Tomato Juice (pg. 85). A juicer is recommended.

Yields: about 4 cups juice

INDEX

67271321R00053